# in the pink
a woman's guide to being a girl

## Ramona Prater

### Edited by Brook Blander

ebonyLotus Creatives | Xpressions and Publishing
www.ebonylotus.com
Rochester  Michigan

Copyright© 2010 Ramona Prater

All rights reserved. No part of this may be reproduced in any form or by any means, electronic or mechanical, including photocopying, recording, or by any information storage and retrieval system, without permission in writing from the publisher and or author.

ISBN: 0-9767592-2-5

Cover design: Niara Innovations Design Studio, Michigan

Published in the United States of America

Table of Contents

Foreword					7
Introduction				10
Damsels In Distress			13
Put Your Lips Together		22
Power of the Neck			26
The Way Up is Down			29
Project YOU!				33
About The Author			41

# Foreword
## DeAngela Lockett

I was more than anxious to help bring this project to life. Ramona and I happened to bump into each other after a chance meeting. We hadn't even seen each other for 7 years, easily. And when we do bump into each other it is 5 AM in the morning! We were ecstatic to see each other, and converged to catch up over coffee and grits!

We chatted, and as anybody that knows a 'Prater' can attest to the fact that they are hilarious separately, but together with another nut (i.e. myself) and you have a riot of a time. As we laughed about Pepper, the demon-dog, old relationships and new ones alike, this book, *In The Pink* was conceived. As we sat there and talked about every issue and scenario that women in and out of relationships face, it was clear to me. "Mo, you need to write a book!" So, she did.

Through career and personal demands, schedule conflicts and writer's block, from children to church, she made time to write this book. Having at all times, each woman, each family and each household in mind that would be affected.

At the time I spoke with Ramona, I had just completed the heartbreak cycle of a past love interest. I was beyond the 'he was a dog' stage and on to the 'you picked him, so what does that say about you' phase. I had analyzed, and reflected and was at a time where I wanted to date, have some fun and explore what was out there, for the new and improved inner me.

As this book began to unfold, I didn't say much to Ramona about what I had personally gone through and how uneasy I was about opening myself to a new relationship or entering the dating scene. The thought of it was tiring to me. So I just listened. And I read. And I listened some more.

Then I had a thought. If the ideals and suggestions in this book were authentic, then I would be a perfect candidate to 'test' some of these theories. So to the lab of life I went. Armed with the pink principles I opened this book while in the writing process and became a student of Pink!

And though the events would take too much time to detail in this foreword, let's just say that within a 1-month period, I have had 2 marriage proposals, 1 serious relationship rekindled and dozens, yes, dozens of dinner invitations. (WARNING: Results may vary.)

I was as shocked as anyone. I couldn't believe that these little things were turning the tables and men were responding to the simplest, Pink Principle - be careful, not to bat too much, you could look like you have something in your eye! (an inside joke; read the book!)

Men are simple creatures and most real men will tell you that. If a woman were to become a student of male behaviors and learn from other women that are making it happen each day, you would be surprised what great man you would attract to your path.

My thought is simple, if you want to learn how to cook, you go get a cookbook with recipes in it. Then you find someone who knows how to cook well. *In The Pink* is your recipe book on relationships and Ramona Prater is a person who knows the anatomy of a man's mind. Take notes, as she teaches you how to Pink your love life for good.

*in the pink*
a woman's guide to being a girl

## Introduction

If I hear another woman tout the phrase "I'm a strong independent woman", I may very well pull out my hair… both the strands that I bought and the ones that I grew! Because if the truth be told, I don't know <u>one</u> independent woman who is not also "independent"… of a MAN!

Since the start of the female revolution in the late 60's and 70's, there has been a slow decline of successful relationships, happy marriages and functional homes. I can remember listening to the theme song of the hit TV show, "Maude" sung by the late Donny Hathaway. He sang of how 'Lady Godiva' was a freedom rider, riding her horse in the buff through the town. In one of the verses he talked about the bra burning movement…and how men were most excited about that! Then, ended the ditty with a hand on your hip, let your backbone slip list of in-your-face adjectives climaxing with **"RIGHT ON MAUDE!!!"**

Whenever I heard that song it worked me into a frenzy of feminine freedom! And I couldn't wait to stand toe-to-toe with any man…and tell him how strong and powerful I was and how I didn't need him! What I didn't realize then is that no man wants another …well, honestly, another man.

There's a reason God made men and women different from each other. We are supposed to balance each other to create the perfect harmonious relationship. I honestly believe the greatest tool that has been used to destroy the American Family was the notion that…<u>women should be equal to men</u>. Now, before you get mad at me ladies. Let me clarify my position and explain what I mean by this.

I DO believe that women should receive equal pay for equal work. And I don't believe women should be treated like property or as if they are less than a man. I know women can make a living, live and exist without a man, raise children successfully and enjoy financial freedom without a man…have a good time and excel in both the world of business and finance *without* a man. But I think it's so much nicer *with*…a MAN!

I've heard women of all ages, socioeconomic and racial backgrounds say… they don't "need" a man, but I know that's not true. I know that GOD made us to want and need each other. I have found that those statements are in fact just a pose; a brave face designed to disguise the hurt, unmet expectations, and broken hearts of women who have yet to meet Mr. Right.

Look, I have been there and that is the reason I'm writing this little book. I want to help us take a look at ourselves. Think for a minute. What if ALL the *good* men are NOT in jail, homosexual, threatened by our success or too short? What if our *attitudes and macho mannerisms* have turned ALL our best prospects off? Let's think about that for a minute, shall we? What if *you* need some work?

Well, if you do…don't worry. Help is on the way! Operating in the "pink" will help you attract a true "blue" man.

In fact I'm so certain that the principles I've written about in this manual will help you attract the man of your dreams… you may as well go try on a few wedding dresses! Are you ready for the best years of LOVE in your life? The best is next, when you operate..."*In The PINK*"!

## Damsels in Distress

Today's woman is anything but the preverbal 'Damsel in Distress'. She is strong, resourceful and competent and able to take care of all kinds of challenges with success. Many times, we seldom have time to think about how it is getting done. All we know is that it needs to be done, so we do it.

Let me be the first to say, being a strong woman is an admirable quality that we should all master…just in case we need those skills. My mother would always say, "Ramona, there is nothing we do better than what we have to do." Thus, the birth of the army of STRONG, <u>INDEPENDENT</u> WOMAN!

With a divorce rate of over 50% and the number of single parent homes at an all time high in this country, many women have become 'independent' and 'strong-willed' by default. Some women have had no choice but to be the heads of the homes, they have to make it happen financially and assume the general traditional responsibility of a man in the absence of a partner to share the load. Before we continue on let's define the various types of "distress" that I'm not talking about; the kind that can be avoided by simply making better choices.

There are women have decided on their own that they will take on "motherhood", without the consent of a man, you know who you are... and you should be ashamed of yourself. What you become is a woman who collects a reluctant check from a man who hates you for 18 years; or a woman who depends on government assistance for the rest of your life instead of for a bridge to take you from bad times to better. I don't think it's fair to you or your children to take on motherhood without the ability to care for them, either emotionally or financially. I have to take a moment to address this group of women, those who take on a victim role after they engage in a consensual sexual act with a partner without birth control...a baby is the result. **YOU** make the decision to have a baby, then you force a male to pay child support and the rest of us to give over a portion of our taxes for a child we had nothing to do with for at least 18 years.

I will always maintain this position. It is the woman's job to make sure **SHE** does not conceive, especially in liaisons that are CASUAL in nature. If you barely know a man's last name...why would you have unprotected sex with him??? If you've never met his folks or have been out to dinner with him...if you know you're his side dish and that he's in another relationship with someone else...if he only comes through when the moon is in the sky...if he has never "shown" that he loves you...forget about him saying it because talk is cheap. Why would you expect a man who only slept with you to want to father a child with you? Why are you on Jerry Springer, Maury...or writing letters to Steve Harvey asking why **HE** won't take care of his responsibility????

Wise up ladies, start thinking **PINK!** In the advent of an unwanted pregnancy, it is **YOU**, the woman, who stands to bare the brunt of the responsibility. Women, where is your pride? Don't chase a man after the fact to take care of a child that he never wanted. Truth be told he never wanted you. It may sound harsh but it's a truth meant to heal. **PREVENT** pregnancy in **YOUR** body. If a man isn't willing to give you *his last name too*...forget the idea of having his baby. Good Grief!!!! The Church says you can prevent pregnancy by practicing abstinence, which is a novel, moral concept when it works. But my mom who was a Christian gave us this advice "Young women who are living for Jesus, don't have premarital sex….however, if you find yourself burning with passion , find a reliable source of birth control? The moral consequences," she reminded us, we would have to pay. She went on to say that there is no need to bring any more children in the world without the benefit of a solid family structure" She reminded us often how she had 14 children by a man who loved her and shared both the dream of a big family and the process to fruition from the beginning of their courtship. My mom would brag about how she had a husband who loved her and worked 38 years at Ford Motor company without missing a day to take care of her and their children. She warned us never to put <u>ourselves</u> in the position where you had to question your child's paternity!!! In short, take the precautions, ask the necessary questions with the male you're engaging in sexual intercourse with BEFORE the issue of an unwanted pregnancy is an issue.

There are myriad reasons why single moms are reentering the dating world…and while you may find a mate in your current situation will it be the best mate for you? And how long will it last?

Next up for examination… the growing number of grown "boys" more commonly known as "momma's boys" produced by an army of "distressed" women who have misplaced their affection towards their children. It's my observation that these poor children are treated like the men in their mom's life in the absence of a grown man and a healthy relationship. These little boys are showered with both affection and material things from the moment they leave the womb. They are not trained to do household chores, manage money, to handle rejection or receive anything but praise. They are not raised to earn money but rather given anything they want in exchange for their affection …literally bought by their mothers. They've been constantly told how good looking they are and how they are God's gift the world. They grow up not being able to hold a job, not needing security independent of their moms who let them know they can

ALWAYS come home to live or worse yet, never leave. They can't maintain a loving relationship with a woman because all they know how to do is taking…from the first women in their lives. These adult boys will end up searching for a woman who will replicate the relationship they have with their moms. They have little more than sex to offer as adults in relationships because that's all they're equipped to do. They have no real skill set, they are emotionally undeveloped and overall unprepared to function in the world. In some cases, these men will excel in sports or any other thing that requires cheerleading, praise and adulation. The final product is a whole batch of worthless boys posing as men. Sound mean? Think of your daughters if you won't think of yourselves out here in the dating world. Honestly, one of my worst fears with regard to my daughter dating in the future is her being attached to a "man' like the one I've just described. My hope is that she has so much "PINK" in her, she'll pick up on those traits and tell- tell signs early enough to flee.

Ladies, have you ever dated a guy like this? Worst yet, are you raising a man like this?

Newsflash, you are if you're sacrificing all of yourself for your child, and putting your needs behind all of his. Whether it is all the practices, all of the latest new clothes and video games etc, you may be on a road of parental destruction of which there is no return. I don't mean the usual sacrifices we all make as parents to rear a productive members of society. I mean those of you who have spoiled your boys to the point where he is no good. Now how do you know this? Well to begin with, if your son is an adult and still lives with you…you failed him. If he drives a car that you pay the note on, madam you're failing your son. If he has children that you take care of…you've failed your child. If you still buy him clothes or take care of him, you have failed both him and any potential mate of his. You've failed him by not preparing him to be a man, a husband and father. I have 7 brothers and I can still remember my mom waking them up early on weekday mornings in the summer. She would make them put on dress clothes and hit the streets on foot or by bus to look for a job.

She would say as long as my husband gets up at 4am to leave for work...every young man in this house will do the same thing...no man is going to be able to lie around her house. I remember thinking how hard my mom was on my brothers. She made them, and all of us for that matter, learn how to balance a checkbook. She taught us the value of a "good name", a biblical principle that promotes the value of GOOD CREDIT! She made us sit and listen to her when she had to make payment arrangements with the utility companies if ever she and dad were short. She made all of us take turns sitting with her in the kitchen while she washed dishes and cooked before we were required to do the task without her.

My mother would offer this explanation when we would ask her why, (and trust me we did), "I'm trying to raise men and women, who will be valuable citizens, husbands and wives." She said to my brothers specifically when they would protest. "I'm hard on you because you have to be a husband, father and head of house one day" I'm happy to report that ALL seven of my brothers have met and exceeded her goal.

My mother has been dead almost 20 years but she prepared all of her children while we were young to not only live, but thrive without her. Moms, the best ways to judge the job you've done rearing your son is how and *if* he can live on his own without you. He will never be anyone's husband or man as long as he is your "boy".

**Ladies, MEN are MADE...not BORN!**

Cut the apron strings and prepare yourself for a chance with a relationship with a grown man... he's out there and you're worth it. Perhaps previous men didn't want to compete with your unhealthy relationship with your son. Again if this truth hurts, its ok, the same truth has the power to break the cycle of dysfunction and heal.

There is another group of women who are successful and financially secure. They've completed their education, have advanced degrees, excel in their career fields and many other goals... putting having a husband and family on hold...behind goals that they can actually control the variables in, to some degree.

At some point or another I've been a combination of one or two of these groups. We'll go into that in greater detail in a moment. But for now, let's go on to the next group.

The last group of women is the beautiful model types or the frumpy, plump women with an overall bad attitude. My bootleg degree in psychology says they're either mad at the world for the 'hating them for being beautiful' or mad at everyone around them for not 'accepting them for their perceived shortcomings'. In my opinion usually those are their thoughts concerning themselves more than external projections towards them. They project those negative vibes out into the world, and others, especially men, pick them up and interpret them as overall 'ugliness'.

This is the most critical of all groups, because without a serious attitude overhaul, they could end up miserable and alone for a lifetime, But it doesn't have to be that way.

With all the responsibilities that have been heaped on our plates it's no wonder we've lost most our girlish qualities. These are the qualities that are the most attractive to men. If you're a woman who speaks often and openly about how much you don't need a man…. Newsflash! The likelihood of you getting one is greatly diminished.

I am around women who always brag about how much money they make, how they can fix their own cars, hang dry wall and buy their own homes. These women have adapted to the song, 'Independent Women' by R&B female group, Destiny's Child as an anthem.

What they fail to realize is that the song, though wonderfully performed and smartly written – should be enjoyed in large part as entertainment. If I may, I would like to change the words of the song a little to say, 'all the women independent throw your (ring less) hands up at me' (smile).

I have the utmost respect for Destiny's Child and I'm sure they meant the song to be a nod to all the women that are doing their thing in a man's world. I'm cool with that, because when I heard the song 'Cater to You' just a few CD's later I know they have a real understanding of how relationships flow.

Consider this ladies…why would you buy your own clothes, shoes, purses, gas or even gum, for that matter, when there's a handsome guy perfectly willing to do it for you? I'm **NOT** suggesting that we should be gold diggers…NOT at all!

But I do suggest firmly that a woman who "allows" a man to be a man in a relationship (by being a girl) will rarely 'have' to open her wallet. This is a reciprocal thing though. A man you spoil will typically pull out all the stops to spoil you back. However, every man doesn't merit the all out "pink" treatment. Only those who are true "blue" do…we'll get into that further a little later on in the book, right now let's keep the focus on us!

To begin with, getting back to exhibiting your girlish qualities is the first step on the road to a balanced relationship. To understand that all men need to feel needed by a woman is the foundation of the "pink" principle, when you constantly proclaim to the world all that you don't <u>need.</u>

Why would you expect a creature that enjoys being 'needed' to respond to you? That's a formula for insanity … and it explains everything that's wrong with regard to the current relationship crisis.

The idea of the 'Damsel in Distress', or the girl who needs to be 'rescued', is born from this principle. The knight in shining armor always showed up to assist the damsel who 'needed' him.

It was the moment he shined. It is in this moment that he feels his sense of purpose rises to the occasion and saves the day. In it he senses, "this is my time to tap into all the man I am for the woman of my desires."

Consequently, she desperately falls for him. Men rely on this principle in the art of war/love.

Can you imagine a modern woman with a lot of mouth in the middle of the hypothetical woods lost and alone with her GPS system...boldly declaring, "I'll get out of here on my own steam without help from anyone! I'm not frail and helpless. I can figure this out on my own. I have a Master's degree, I own my own business, I make BIG money, I'm the director of my company, and so on... so this is nothing." Meanwhile, all the suitors pick up her crotchety, male signal and repeatedly pass her up for someone who actually WANTS help!

As tragic as this scenario sounds, it happens every day. I see it all too often. These same women although they are usually very intelligent have bought into the very popular new world doctrine 'anything you can do I can do better' feminist movement philosophy, but they should consider this...even the super feminist poster child for independent women – Gloria Steinem – got MARRIED!

We, all of us girls, if not wholly, at least in part, need to get back to dropping our handkerchief and batting our eyelashes (in a manner of speaking). Even if we know the answers to all the questions in the universe, even if you are a certified genius, would it kill you to ask your boyfriend where you should go to get your oil changed? Or who should prepare your taxes? Would it take so much from you to ask him what he'd like to see you wear today? Or what you should you cook/order for dinner occasionally? What you would accomplish in applying these little questions through the day would pay off like the lottery in the evening! (wink) and throughout the years.

A woman on the road to finding the girl that lives within is on a truly remarkable journey, a journey that begins with divorcing all the modern day principles she hears in the media, popular movies and music. A woman who will dare to believe that even the most modern of men still desire and appreciate a woman who is all 'girl'.

Take some of my favorite American actresses, for example…

I worship the quicksand, Bette Davis and Joan Crawford walked on. I loved their movies. And their performances, well… they scared the spit out of most of the leading men in both their professional and personal lives!

Herein lays the problem. A ballsy, high-spirited, overly opinionated, hell on wheels woman is great to watch on TV or listen to on the radio…but no one wants to live in the house with her. Bette Davis was even quoted as saying, 'she never found a man that was strong enough to stand up to her.' Loosely translated, 'she couldn't find a man who wanted to deal with a woman acting like a man.'

Who would…? She, Joan Crawford and Vivian Lee's character in *Gone with the Wind*…Scarlet O'Hara ended up ALONE.

*a woman's guide to being a girl*

## Put Your Lips Together!

This segment of the book is written from personal experience. I was born in June; my last name is "prater" which is the noun of the root word "prate. It is a verbal connotation. Without saying to much more, let me just say... I talk A LOT! So I've been told from everyone by my kindergarten teachers to my ex- husbands!

I have to put that out there just in case you may have been thinking I'm writing this little book from a tower of perfection...hardly. I was taught these lessons from my mom as a child but mastered them through trial an error...especially this section.

Women can out talk men every day and twice on Sundays! That's a natural fact, so when it comes to an argument...er; discussion men will either avoid it like the plague or get in a few quick stingers and run for their lives!!!

I'm reminded of this couple who used to live across the balcony from me in my apartment a few years ago. This couple would go at it faithfully in the most spirited "discussions" that lasted well into the early hours of the morning. It was quite entertaining to listen to; in fact my sister, Dorcas, and I would grab a cup of coffee, settle in and keep score... but believe me *Jimmy* was no match for *Shemeka!!!*

She would call him everything but a child of God, in decibel levels that would attract dogs from as far away as Ohio! She could recite all that she did for him on a regular basis from:

*"Frying chicken for him while he worked the third shift, buying his weed for him and his buddy's to smoke, cooking, cleaning and raising his kids from another woman!!!"*

All Jimmy could do is fit in a 2 word *"explicative"* here and there, but the funniest thing was listening to Jimmy trying to get a word in edgewise because Shemeka... was a lightening fast wordsmith!

What I learned from that experience...and my experience with my ex-husband is that all woman want from men during these heated exchanges are love, reassurance and or security and instead of this need being manifested by simple request...a lack of education and experience causes some of us to do all the things that would DRIVE the object of our affection AWAY!

Shemeka's verbal tantrum only made her increasingly anxious and agitated. She never got the response she wanted from Jimmy so as crazy as it sounds, she continued to take out her disappointment and hurt on him. Sadly, this is what happens when most people argue. Hurt people usually hurt people.

The solution to this is as simple as putting your lips together. The adage that goes "if you don't have anything nice to say, don't say anything at all" should be applied here. I believe the biggest mistake we make in confrontation is not *"**owning the emotion**"* therefore causing the other person to react defensively rather than address your concern.

For example, if Shemeka was upset about Jimmy coming in late every evening, she could begin the discussion with ... *"honey, I feel unimportant, unloved and low on your priority list when you come in late"*. Jimmy would be more likely to apologize and or sympathize with her state of being when given an understanding of how his action effected the woman he loves.

The traditional method of confrontation, which actually just means a "face to face encounter", did not work very well with Shemeka or in your house for that matter... may sound something like this.

*"Why are you constantly coming in this house late? Who were you with? I'm not going to be sitting around here waiting while you're doing God only knows what out in the streets! Who do you think you are? Who do you think I am? I'm no fool! There's nothing open after midnight except a woman's legs!!" etc...*

There's only one way any man worth his salt would answer that kind of barrage of words...with a couple of verbal "two pieces" followed by a complete shut down. Men just can't handle verbal confrontations from women... they generally can't go pound for pound and blow for blow with women when it comes to words...some men who <u>literally</u> can't take the barrage will react or defend themselves with violence.

I can almost hear some of you readers gasping! Is Ramona suggesting that men have the right to hit women???? NO! Absolutely not... I am, however, suggesting that if you don't want to find yourself on the receiving end of a knuckle sandwich... you should stay out of a Man's face with a lot of angry hateful words... you will just be asking for it.

Those of you mouthy women who haven't been hit already, you're lucky, but don't push your luck further. Learn now how to **"put your lips together!"**

State your case sweetly, begin with owning the emotion quickly. Say how you feel behind his actions as you head into the kitchen to make him a snack..."work out the rest," as my mother would say, "in the evening hours". (wink) The benefits will be reminiscent of hitting a never-ending JACKPOT! Trust me.

When we own the emotion in a confrontation, we disarm the person allowing them to focus on how whatever they've done effects us, rather than jump on the defense.

My children are quick to use what they call their "I" words when they deal with me.

They learned this version of owning the emotion called **"I messages"** in their elementary school. They'll say things like… Mommy "I" feel sad when you say turn the TV off early even on Friday nights… or "my feelings were hurt when you put me on punishment for not getting more words right on my spelling test, because I did the best I could".

It's the cutest thing… and sometimes, because of their approach I'll even change my mind.

When we practice being "pink" in relationships", we learn that being right is less important than being heard and most importantly understood!

When we approach a man with sweet, confident, non-threatening and quiet spirit…we're much more likely to experience more favorable results.

So, *take your hands off your hips, stop letting your backbone slip, take your shoes off, get to the kitchen and Put your lips together!!!* (Smile) Your man is going to be like putty in your loving hands!

*in the pink*
a woman's guide to being a girl

## The Power of the Neck

My mother, Joyce Prater, married my dad, Terry, at the tender age of 19 years old. My dad was 21. They were married in Texas just before my dad was shipped off to the army. Nine months later, my older sister Donna was born! The first of fourteen children, seven girls and seven boys! Our upbringing and our home was a pretty typical and was closer to the TV families of Cosby/Brady Bunch experience than that of The Good Times/All in the Family variety.

I said that to say we had a solid family structure complete with the occasional dog… usual arguments, punishments, whippings, etc.

But our home was filled with laughter as well. My parents both came from broken homes and were determined to have a "big happy family" and they pulled out all the stops to make that a reality.

My mother was a master "neck" she made it very clear who the **BIG BAD WOLF** was in our house…it was my DAD! But she never had any trouble getting *anything* she wanted. As an adult myself now, I am amazed at what a tight ship my mother ran.

The corporation that was the Prater house was run not unlike any other fortune five hundred company. We all had specific duties and responsibilities so the house ran like a machine.

On occasion, my dad would blow his top about one thing or another and I can remember my mom, who was quite feisty in her own right, would hold her position and keep her composition throughout his passionate, mobile display about whatever he was upset about at the time. She would listen attentively and nod her head agreeing with everything he said. She sometimes would get up, mid rant and begin to fix him fried chicken or a sandwich...all while saying softly "you're right, Honey".

I can't tell you how many times I heard my father forbid my mother to do something from buying a new car to going back to school or letting one of us do something in school. I remember wanting to cut my hair or start wearing make-up, (ideas my father didn't even entertain less alone agree to).

But my mom, while in conference with us both, would say "Ramona, your dad is right, you are still too young." But as soon as he got up and left the room triumphantly, she'd say "Mo, let me work on him for you." Come morning, I got what I wanted...and have been cutting my hair and wearing make up ever since.

I think I was about sixteen years old before my sisters and I circled my mother and asked her what her secret power was...what was that special something that worked like magic on my dad? It was then that I first heard the expression "Girls, your dad is the head of this house, but I'm the neck that turns it," she went on to say. Have you ever seen a head function without a neck? How would it look from side to side, or lift up or down? A head couldn't even sneeze properly without the agility a neck provides.

Sure, it's an understated part of the anatomy often covered up by collars, scarves or ties...but it's no less important to the function of the body...dare I say an essential part of the body.

I believe GOD made the parallel truth about the neck and the role of a woman to illustrate the simplicity of submission. That it's not the slave like perception once thought of by some feminist, but the key to balance in relationships and overall happiness.

My father would be the first to tell you that though he wore the pants in our house…it was my mothers' wishes that ended up being the rule. But not through a willful combative, cantankerous attitude…as a new colt that needs to be broken, rather a sweet agreeable manner. In the same way a neck never bosses up on the head…but still gets its way! DUH!

It is the *"neck"* that provides all of the head's agility and mobility. It is the *"neck"* that allows the head to stand erect and proud. It is the same *"neck"* that won't allow the head to hang too low too long without considerable discomfort!

Finally, it is that same neck that would be worthless "independent" of its Head….and vice versa!

The way I see it the strength of a **strong** woman lies in her ability to function as a *"neck"*.

## The Way Up is Down

So much has been written and said about the "s" word, I hardly know where to start. For most modern women it can be added to the list of swear words or other unmentionable things like chastity belts!!!! Just the thought of that makes me want to give up my first birthday cake!

Similar emotions are stirred in modern women by the word...dare I say it...**_submission._**

If you haven't put this book down after that last line, we're in good shape. That's because I, like you think the notion of walking two steps behind a man, or keeping your head bowed in his presence is retarded!

Actually I think some man with a warped self-esteem perverted this principle to serve his underdeveloped ego. You've heard of the Napoleonic complex, wherein men of smaller statue, whether physical or emotional, feel the need to possess larger scale items or overcompensate for their insecurities by adapting a superior mentality.

They will always strip others down to make themselves appear more significant, rulers like Adolph Hitler should be the poster child for this syndrome.

And on the other side of the same coin so should **_some_** leaders of the **_church_**...but that's another book, coming soon.... I promise.

Submission, by design improves relationships. So we won't throw the baby out, with the dirty bath water just because some crazy people have distorted the meaning of submission.

I'll give you a few examples of submission that work in various relationships.

In every corporation there is a C.E.O, C.F.O, President, Vice President, Department Head, Manager, Supervisors, Team Leaders and so on. In the same way in the military you'll have Generals, Colonels, Lieutenants, Corporals, Privates... etc. These are positions designed to work within the principle of submission.

Each rank has another person that reports to he/she someone who submits to that authority, to accomplish order.

Order is the precursor of peace and the absence of order is chaos. Another example can be found in nature, there are many but this one is the most poignant for me.

On the darkest nights the moon lights the earth with its entire splendor and it's in its greatest glory! At night all eyes are on the moon as we look to it for light...that is until the SUN comes up! I didn't realize this until very recently but while the Sun is up during the day providing heat and light for the earth, the moon never stops shining... as great as its light is, it's no match for the Sun, the lesser light must give way to the greater light...but it is no less important.

In the same way there will always be the one power that will give way to another power. It's a marriage of different levels of powers that is designed to produce successful, harmonious results. Women will never be equal physically with men. There is a variance of strengths between the two sexes for a divine reason, but when there is mutual respect between men and women the differences work.

Ladies you will always receive the best from your men when you resist the urge to challenge everything he says, even when what they say sounds like backwards Chinese! In fact, ESPECIALLY when it sounds like backwards Chinese...cause if you don't want to end up in a backwards Chinese mess... resist the madness. Before you close the book, let me explain.

The way up *really is down*. We've gone over the principles of *the power of the neck*, and *putting your lips together* but this principle illustrates where the two ends meet in the middle. I can't tell you how many scary propositions I've heard from my sweetheart in my relationship from putting a big ole ugly bark-a-lounger reclining chair in the middle of my tastefully decorated living room, to suggesting we quit our jobs, sell all of our belongings and move out of state.

As the words were leaving his mouth and landing on my ears, I could feel my blood pressure pulsing behind my eyeballs. But I resisted the urge to say "Are you smoking crack!" and instead said this, in the case of the recliner, " ok!"

I said *"that's a great idea. You deserve a place of your own to sit in this house...a place that no one will be allowed to sit in but you. Let's run the furniture store right now!"* After walking around the store for about thirty minutes looking at hideous chairs, I began to stray over into the chaise lounge and chair and a half section of the store. I began to use adjectives like *"strong"*, *"durable"*, *"distinguished"*, and *"sexy"* when I referred to the look and overall design of the chairs that I preferred for him. I asked him to sit down in the ones that matched *my* current living room decor and commented, in a matter of fact way, how good he looked in them. I also suggested that we pick up a beautiful large serving tray that I could serve him sandwiches and ice cold beer on while he watched all his favorite sporting events.

Without saying much more we were walking out of the store with the exact chair *I* wanted and my sweetheart was none the wiser, but equally happy! In the case of moving out of state, I just responded, "Honey, I'd trust you to lead me...even to the ends of the earth" the next day I showed him the resignation letter I'd written to my boss for his approval along with copy detailing a moving sale I would post in the weekend classified ads that begin in big bold letters...**EVERYTHING MUST GO!!!**

Somehow seeing everything in black and white...prompted a subtle change of heart. We never moved his new chair, let alone our entire household.

P.S...
*The lovemaking on the nights of these incredible ideas that my darling makes...well, it's like no other negotiation tactic known in the art of war... so be creative and take the way up is down principle <u>literally</u> in your sex life and watch the floodgates fly open for you! On your knees girls!!! (* ***Smile****)*

Remember when you want your way... let him take the high road and you take the LOW road and you'll get what's best for you "both" all the time.

*in the pink*
a woman's guide to being a girl

## Project YOU!

Throughout the chapters of this book we've talked about all the many ways your partner will benefit from your PINK transformation. But let's just say, we've saved the best benefit for last, the way you will experience the best in your life as a woman… from being a 'girl'.

When I was a child, I was recited the nursery rhyme about little girls being sugar, spice and everything…nice! It made me smile inside to feel proud of this 'movement' called female.

There is indeed something sweet and sunny about the concept of girls. I'm reminded of, Melanie, the character in one of my favorite movies, 'Gone with the Wind'. Hamilton, played by Olivia De'Havilland, was the complete opposite of the main character, Scarlet O'Hara, played by Vivian Leigh. Scarlet was the bold brazing, in your face, "Pistol" of a woman who by comparison – was much more interesting than the meek, feminine, mousy character of Melanie. But in the end, it was Melanie who won the heart of the man of *"both"* their dreams.

There's even a line in the movie that refers to Starlet's behavior during a big barbeque. The scene is set as she was flirting with every guy in attendance to get the attention of her target beau, Ashley Wilkes, who happened to be engaged to Melanie at the time. Two other girls at the party who were observing her actions remarked, "Well, men may flirt with girls like that…but they don't marry them."

Well, I don't know if their take on the situation is entirely true. Perhaps there was a little salted sugar born out of how Scarlet *worked the room*. But I do believe there is a delicate balance between harmless, confidence and transparent, contrived charm.

The way I see it, your man should think of you as medicine…a balm that soothes everything that ails him. You should represent peaceful, sweet and 'sunny' things in his life. I know this may sound a bit saccharin but it's true all the same.

I don't know if you've noticed but lately when I go into schools to speak, or concert halls for shows or even encountering young women in the streets…I've noticed the most uninviting looks on the faces of these *ladies*!

It's as if having a sourpuss look on your face is the new, hot fashion accessory. How can any woman expect a man to approach them when they tout a look and demeanor that reads, 'CLOSED'.

The origin of the laws of attraction can be traced all the way back to the 'good book' in a passage that reads, *if a man wants friends, he must first show himself to be friendly.* Darling, this is not even rocket science.

If you're thinking, 'well, you don't know what I've been through. I have been through this or that and that's why I am sour with the world.' Well, I am not trying to trivialize your troubles or experiences but – everyone has had them. You're not special. You have however, experienced LIFE! Which is, at its best, just mediocre sometimes. A better way to look at each new day would be to cherish every one above ground…as a good day! So no matter what, rejoice anyway…okay!!?

You see, having an improved attitude will make you feel better about yourself and it will make him feel good about himself. Research has shown that many acts of infidelity are not born in lust…but rather in how the other person makes you feel about yourself.

Providing an atmosphere that breeds a sense of pride and appreciation in your relationship that makes your man feel like beating his chest and roaring like a lion is your best insurance for a long-term healthy monogamous relationship. The benefits you'll reap are endless.

I'm not saying that you'll never have conflict in your life, marriage or relationship, but when you do, you'll have the proper attitude and skill set to face and overcome them successfully. People with positive dispositions about life attract positive people and relationships.

WARNING! The 'pink' tips in this book are only to be used on men that are 'true blue'. One of the many things my mother told me that I still remember today with all clarity was something she said when I was about 10 years old. "Ramona, would you like to marry a doctor?" I'd say with enthusiasm, "Sure!" Then she'd ask, "What about a lawyer? Would you like to marry a lawyer, Ramona?" I'd wildly say, "Yes!"

Then she would say, "Then you should go to medical school or law school. You'll find plenty of doctors and lawyers there." In short, she was saying, you need to BE and or HAVE the qualities that you're looking for. A good man will never want anything lower than himself for anything more than an overnight visit. You can forget about seeing daylight with him in your arms, unless he's a vampire or cat burglar!!!!

Now in the event that the man you've been keeping company with is not a man of integrity, not serious about at least exploring a life with you, not treating you with kindness and respect, not giving you ear to your dreams, and or ideas about your life and only seeing you when it's convenient for him….in short he's not interested in you! No problem! Don't hold that against him, but you need to be making your way towards a man that is true blue'.

Project "you" is the part of the **"pink process"** that prompts us to take a long, hard, honest look at ourselves in the mirror and from within. It's the hardest but the most liberating part of our pink journey. Ladies don't get sensitive on me now… but it's time for a little tough LOVE. I'll begin with the group of women who are overweight, at least 30 pounds over their ideal body weight; The clinical definition of obesity. Well not only is being overweight a threat to your health but it's generally unattractive to most men. Don't react yet, please, just hear me out. On the health front more women die from heart disease and diabetes in this country than murders, suicides and car accidents combined. These common diseases are often commonly associated with being overweight. Ladies, I know every woman will not be a cosmopolitan cover girl. I certainly am not. In reality I believe some women especially in the fashion and entertainment industry are on the other end of the weight spectrum and are just as unhealthy. And in some cultures, the more curves you have the better, but being curvy and being overweight are two distantly different things. It's my belief that a lot of well meaning comedians and entertainers have enabled women to believe that it's okay to be a "BIG GIRL", boosting a lot of overweight women's self esteem and proclaiming beauty to a group of women long overlooked by Madison Ave and the general fashion world. But here's what I've discovered… most of those comedians and entertainers who profess to LOVE BIG WOMEN, DO NOT have BIG wives and girlfriends. The whole BIG GIRL thing is just good for their reputation with a huge (no pun intended) demographic, and enormous ticket sales booster. Likewise, heavy women who claim they are happy… really are not. If you're overweight right now… are you? The only proof I offer to back that statement is the multi-billion dollar diet industry in this country alone; A country full of obese people".

I had to begin this last principle with that paragraph to illustrate the following point. If you've been saying I don't have a man because I'm a "lil" fat. Be honest… are you too heavy? Have a *few good men* passed on you and you dismiss the false starts with the following excuses …"he was probably gay"…"he just likes white girls or black girls"…or, I love this one… "He's just intimidated by me".  If the answer is yes… deal with that honestly.  Could it be that you were heavier than his preference? Even if that's not the reason, how about eliminating that from the equation. If you've been making excuses about why you're not at your ideal weight…Stop. If you've been telling yourself that your prince charming is going to like you just the way you are… consider how slim the odds are. With all due respect, you never see fat centerfolds or supermodels…you know, the kind of women men "pin up". If you've been plain ole eating too much…STOP IT! Start eating right and get some exercise.

If you're at your at your ideal weight and your outside appearance is healthy and packaged well… wonderful, but if you still haven't found your "true blue" mate, perhaps you need an internal overhaul.

You've heard the phrase; "attitude is everything" well this is so true when attracting the opposite sex.  A confident, not conceded, persona mixed with a fun loving lady-like spirit is attractive to everyone…especially men. I know different men like various things in women, but generally speaking, gentlemen are attracted to ladies. If you're a woman that we spoke of earlier in the book that has an overall "closed" persona, if you wear a blank or sour look on your face more than a pleasant smile, if you emit a polished yet uninviting, unpleasant…"strong women" vibe to the world and men at large…. YOU need a pink makeover.

One of the biggest turn-offs to any man, modern or otherwise, is a woman who can't cook. I can almost feel you dropping the book here…but hang on, we're almost finished. When I speak to women who don't cook, women who say "I never go into my kitchen" or "I don't even boil water" thinking that's cute… I often notice these women do not have boyfriends or husbands. It's no surprise to me. I've referenced making your sweetheart a sandwich when contention is brewing a few times already to illustrate this ancient point.

The way to a man's heart really is through his stomach. No matter what time you feel contention brewing a good meal takes the edge off. Even if you're not a gourmet chef... a good ole sandwich works as well as Filet Mignon! But get creative work on the craft of cooking. Experiment with recipes and even ask him to shop for ingredients and cook with you sometimes. It makes for great together time. Providing an atmosphere that is warm, inviting, comforting and a refuge from the world is essential to any healthy relationship. Trust me, if you're looking to pad your stats... the moment you finish reading this book, buy a cookbook.

Here begins the work out! As with any journey of self-help, we have to begin with confession or admission. If you are a reader who is feeling resistant to what you've just read, let me offer you this as a peace offering. There is a biblical principle that states..." with the mouth confession is made unto salvation". Loosely translated, that means once you admit what is wrong....you can get help. It works in hospital ER rooms, you have to go through "admitting" or tell the staff what's "wrong" with you...before you can receive any treatment. This principle has been adopted and is effective in NA and AA twelve step programs. The first step being to stand up and "confess" ( ie: My name is _____ and I'm a _____.) It works here too. The road to getting "pink" begins with honestly identifying where you are on the road. Perhaps you're more "red" or "burgundy". Maybe your hue resembles a light "blue". But no matter where you are in the spectrum... to get that "pink place" we need to access where we are now. Take a minute for quiet introspective. Decide whether or not your current plan of attack has been working for you and if you're willing to try another approach ... a "pink" approach! The choice is yours. Go ahead and use the space below to <u>honestly</u> access/confess where you are and want to be.

Ladies, we will never rise above our confession. So write down your dream, give yourself a real plan of attack and timeline to complete it. Post it somewhere that you can recite it everyday (I like my bathroom mirror) and watch yourself become the image of your daily confession. I can tell you with a reasonable assurance that applying these principles will only change your life for the better. Applying these principles will not only make you more attractive, but attract only the best groups of men to your "batting lashes" and "dropping hankies" smile! Men that want a real woman, a woman who is all girl!

I wish you all Pink Dreams!!!

*Ramona*

## Ramona Prater
Author of "In The Pink"

Born and raised in Northwest Detroit to a family of 16…7 brothers and 6 sisters, Ramona was reared with the values of family at the forefront of any goal or achievement.

Ramona believes that if she accomplishes what her parents did in her home…it will make her among the wealthiest people in earth.

And that is to create an atmosphere where learning, laughing, love, truth and honor…produce law abiding civically responsible citizens in the community.

After working in the media in some form or another it is Ramona's firm beliefs that we can trace all of the ills in our society to imbalances at home… no matter the make up of the family.

Ramona was educated in the Detroit Public Schools system and learned the art of Radio Television Broadcast at Oakland University, Henry Ford Community college in Dearborn and Specs Howard School Broadcast.

She has worked in just about all areas of media from commercial advertising, Christian television hosting and production, TV news as a producer reporter for NBC in Raleigh, NC to TV news producer for WDIV TV 4 here in Detroit.

Ramona now wakes up Detroit every weekday morning with live, news, traffic and weather updates…

During the Steve Harvey Morning Show on MIX 92.3! and FM 98 WJLB

And keeps the city spiritually uplifted on Sunday Afternoons…during her all gospel Sunday shift…before heading to MIX's sister station WJLB to co-host their weekly community affairs program…

"Girl Bye" Sunday Evenings at 7pm with three of her co workers! Listen live at www.fm98wjlb.com

Ramona enjoys working up a sweat by running, tennis and kickboxing and hanging out with her family and three children
Justin, a senior at the University of Michigan, Kobe a budding Hockey player, and Maya the next Hanna Montana!

# Questions and Activities

## The Introduction

What are /were your qualifications for a man? (i.e. height, weight, age, complexion, income)

_____
_____
_____
_____
_____
_____
_____
_____
_____
_____
_____
_____
_____
_____
_____
_____
_____
_____
_____
_____
_____
_____
_____
_____
_____
_____
_____

## Try It!

After reading the chapter, Damsels in Distress, begin to change the way to respond to men. Take on the posture of a damsel and write down the way men respond to you.

# Questions and Activities

## Damsels in Distress

When you think the relationships that you've had or wanted-did you ever play the damsel in distress? If so, what was the result of this interaction? If not, can you identify a time when you could have allowed the gentleman to feel needed? And what was your attitude, in both body language and verbally?

_____
_____
_____
_____
_____
_____
_____
_____
_____
_____
_____
_____
_____
_____
_____
_____
_____
_____
_____
_____
_____
_____
_____
_____
_____
_____
_____

## Try It!

After reading the chapter, Damsels in Distress, begin to change the way to respond to men. Take on the posture of a damsel and write down the way that men respond to you.

# Questions and Activities

## Put Your Lips Together

There is only one question that needs to be asked here...Do YOU talk too much?

_____
_____
_____
_____
_____
_____
_____
_____
_____
_____
_____
_____
_____
_____
_____
_____
_____
_____
_____
_____
_____
_____
_____
_____
_____
_____
_____

## Try It!

When you are having a strong disagreement with your partner or you want to communicate something that is bothering you, practice not responding right away. Give yourself some time to think about what is going to come out of your mouth BEFORE you speak!

# Questions and Activities

## The Power of the Neck

What attributes does a 'neck' have that you can equate to a woman's role in a relationship?

_____
_____
_____
_____
_____
_____
_____
_____
_____
_____
_____
_____
_____
_____
_____
_____
_____
_____
_____
_____
_____
_____
_____
_____
_____
_____

## Try It!

Close your eyes and see yourself as the 'neck' in your relationship or the relationship that you would like to be in. Can you see yourself as the support and strength that is steady and secure?

# Questions and Activities

## The Way Up is Down

Before reading the chapter, The Way Up Is Down, how did you define submission? And now?

___

## Try It!

Over the next week, write down incidents where you have been confronted with opportunities to be submissive. Ask yourself the best way you could have handled it. And what you would have done differently, if anything.

# Questions and Activities

## Project You!

Single ladies, what attributes should you be cultivating to make yourself more attractive and able to handle a relationship on a genuine and honest level?

_____
_____
_____
_____
_____
_____
_____
_____
_____
_____
_____
_____
_____
_____
_____
_____
_____
_____
_____
_____
_____
_____
_____
_____
_____

## Try It!

Go back through this book and highlight the things that stuck out to you most. Ask yourself what changes you need to make in order to make your relationship more valuable.

Keep up with In The Pink and other endeavors by Ramona Prater at:

# www.RamonaPrater.com